# Agenda
## 2019–2020

# ESTA AGENDA PERTENECE A:

_____

# 2019

## Enero

| M | T | W | T | F | S | S |
|---|---|---|---|---|---|---|
|   | 1 | 2 | 3 | 4 | 5 | 6 |
| 7 | 8 | 9 | 10 | 11 | 12 | 13 |
| 14 | 15 | 16 | 17 | 18 | 19 | 20 |
| 21 | 22 | 23 | 24 | 25 | 26 | 27 |
| 28 | 29 | 30 | 31 |   |   |   |

## Febrero

| M | T | W | T | F | S | S |
|---|---|---|---|---|---|---|
|   |   |   |   | 1 | 2 | 3 |
| 4 | 5 | 6 | 7 | 8 | 9 | 10 |
| 11 | 12 | 13 | 14 | 15 | 16 | 17 |
| 18 | 19 | 20 | 21 | 22 | 23 | 24 |
| 25 | 26 | 27 | 28 |   |   |   |

## Marzo

| M | T | W | T | F | S | S |
|---|---|---|---|---|---|---|
|   |   |   |   | 1 | 2 | 3 |
| 4 | 5 | 6 | 7 | 8 | 9 | 10 |
| 11 | 12 | 13 | 14 | 15 | 16 | 17 |
| 18 | 19 | 20 | 21 | 22 | 23 | 24 |
| 25 | 26 | 27 | 28 | 29 | 30 | 31 |

## Abril

| M | T | W | T | F | S | S |
|---|---|---|---|---|---|---|
| 1 | 2 | 3 | 4 | 5 | 6 | 7 |
| 8 | 9 | 10 | 11 | 12 | 13 | 14 |
| 15 | 16 | 17 | 18 | 19 | 20 | 21 |
| 22 | 23 | 24 | 25 | 26 | 27 | 28 |
| 29 | 30 |   |   |   |   |   |

## Mayo

| M | T | W | T | F | S | S |
|---|---|---|---|---|---|---|
|   | 1 | 2 | 3 | 4 | 5 |   |
| 6 | 7 | 8 | 9 | 10 | 11 | 12 |
| 13 | 14 | 15 | 16 | 17 | 18 | 19 |
| 20 | 21 | 22 | 23 | 24 | 25 | 26 |
| 27 | 28 | 29 | 30 | 31 |   |   |

## Junio

| M | T | W | T | F | S | S |
|---|---|---|---|---|---|---|
|   |   |   |   |   | 1 | 2 |
| 3 | 4 | 5 | 6 | 7 | 8 | 9 |
| 10 | 11 | 12 | 13 | 14 | 15 | 16 |
| 17 | 18 | 19 | 20 | 21 | 22 | 23 |
| 24 | 25 | 26 | 27 | 28 | 29 | 30 |

## Julio

| M | T | W | T | F | S | S |
|---|---|---|---|---|---|---|
| 1 | 2 | 3 | 4 | 5 | 6 | 7 |
| 8 | 9 | 10 | 11 | 12 | 13 | 14 |
| 15 | 16 | 17 | 18 | 19 | 20 | 21 |
| 22 | 23 | 24 | 25 | 26 | 27 | 28 |
| 29 | 30 | 31 |   |   |   |   |

## Agosto

| M | T | W | T | F | S | S |
|---|---|---|---|---|---|---|
|   |   |   | 1 | 2 | 3 | 4 |
| 5 | 6 | 7 | 8 | 9 | 10 | 11 |
| 12 | 13 | 14 | 15 | 16 | 17 | 18 |
| 19 | 20 | 21 | 22 | 23 | 24 | 25 |
| 26 | 27 | 28 | 29 | 30 | 31 |   |

## Septiembre

| M | T | W | T | F | S | S |
|---|---|---|---|---|---|---|
|   |   |   |   |   |   | 1 |
| 2 | 3 | 4 | 5 | 6 | 7 | 8 |
| 9 | 10 | 11 | 12 | 13 | 14 | 15 |
| 16 | 17 | 18 | 19 | 20 | 21 | 22 |
| 23 | 24 | 25 | 26 | 27 | 28 | 29 |
| 30 |   |   |   |   |   |   |

## Octubre

| M | T | W | T | F | S | S |
|---|---|---|---|---|---|---|
|   | 1 | 2 | 3 | 4 | 5 | 6 |
| 7 | 8 | 9 | 10 | 11 | 12 | 13 |
| 14 | 15 | 16 | 17 | 18 | 19 | 20 |
| 21 | 22 | 23 | 24 | 25 | 26 | 27 |
| 28 | 29 | 30 | 31 |   |   |   |

## Noviembre

| M | T | W | T | F | S | S |
|---|---|---|---|---|---|---|
|   |   |   |   | 1 | 2 | 3 |
| 4 | 5 | 6 | 7 | 8 | 9 | 10 |
| 11 | 12 | 13 | 14 | 15 | 16 | 17 |
| 18 | 19 | 20 | 21 | 22 | 23 | 24 |
| 25 | 26 | 27 | 28 | 29 | 30 |   |

## Diciembre

| M | T | W | T | F | S | S |
|---|---|---|---|---|---|---|
|   |   |   |   |   |   | 1 |
| 2 | 3 | 4 | 5 | 6 | 7 | 8 |
| 9 | 10 | 11 | 12 | 13 | 14 | 15 |
| 16 | 17 | 18 | 19 | 20 | 21 | 22 |
| 23 | 24 | 25 | 26 | 27 | 28 | 29 |
| 30 | 31 |   |   |   |   |   |

# 2020

## Enero

| M | T | W | T | F | S | S |
|---|---|---|---|---|---|---|
|   |   | 1 | 2 | 3 | 4 | 5 |
| 6 | 7 | 8 | 9 | 10 | 11 | 12 |
| 13 | 14 | 15 | 16 | 17 | 18 | 19 |
| 20 | 21 | 22 | 23 | 24 | 25 | 26 |
| 27 | 28 | 29 | 30 | 31 |   |   |

## Febrero

| M | T | W | T | F | S | S |
|---|---|---|---|---|---|---|
|   |   |   |   |   | 1 | 2 |
| 3 | 4 | 5 | 6 | 7 | 8 | 9 |
| 10 | 11 | 12 | 13 | 14 | 15 | 16 |
| 17 | 18 | 19 | 20 | 21 | 22 | 23 |
| 24 | 25 | 26 | 27 | 28 | 29 |   |

## Marzo

| M | T | W | T | F | S | S |
|---|---|---|---|---|---|---|
|   |   |   |   |   |   | 1 |
| 2 | 3 | 4 | 5 | 6 | 7 | 8 |
| 9 | 10 | 11 | 12 | 13 | 14 | 15 |
| 16 | 17 | 18 | 19 | 20 | 21 | 22 |
| 23 | 24 | 25 | 26 | 27 | 28 | 29 |
| 30 | 31 |   |   |   |   |   |

## Abril

| M | T | W | T | F | S | S |
|---|---|---|---|---|---|---|
|   |   | 1 | 2 | 3 | 4 | 5 |
| 6 | 7 | 8 | 9 | 10 | 11 | 12 |
| 13 | 14 | 15 | 16 | 17 | 18 | 19 |
| 20 | 21 | 22 | 23 | 24 | 25 | 26 |
| 27 | 28 | 29 | 30 |   |   |   |

## Mayo

| M | T | W | T | F | S | S |
|---|---|---|---|---|---|---|
|   |   |   |   | 1 | 2 | 3 |
| 4 | 5 | 6 | 7 | 8 | 9 | 10 |
| 11 | 12 | 13 | 14 | 15 | 16 | 17 |
| 18 | 19 | 20 | 21 | 22 | 23 | 24 |
| 25 | 26 | 27 | 28 | 29 | 30 | 31 |

## Junio

| M | T | W | T | F | S | S |
|---|---|---|---|---|---|---|
| 1 | 2 | 3 | 4 | 5 | 6 | 7 |
| 8 | 9 | 10 | 11 | 12 | 13 | 14 |
| 15 | 16 | 17 | 18 | 19 | 20 | 21 |
| 22 | 23 | 24 | 25 | 26 | 27 | 28 |
| 29 | 30 |   |   |   |   |   |

## Julio

| M | T | W | T | F | S | S |
|---|---|---|---|---|---|---|
|   |   | 1 | 2 | 3 | 4 | 5 |
| 6 | 7 | 8 | 9 | 10 | 11 | 12 |
| 13 | 14 | 15 | 16 | 17 | 18 | 19 |
| 20 | 21 | 22 | 23 | 24 | 25 | 26 |
| 27 | 28 | 29 | 30 | 31 |   |   |

## Agosto

| M | T | W | T | F | S | S |
|---|---|---|---|---|---|---|
|   |   |   |   |   | 1 | 2 |
| 3 | 4 | 5 | 6 | 7 | 8 | 9 |
| 10 | 11 | 12 | 13 | 14 | 15 | 16 |
| 17 | 18 | 19 | 20 | 21 | 22 | 23 |
| 24 | 25 | 26 | 27 | 28 | 29 | 30 |
| 31 |   |   |   |   |   |   |

## Septiembre

| M | T | W | T | F | S | S |
|---|---|---|---|---|---|---|
|   | 1 | 2 | 3 | 4 | 5 | 6 |
| 7 | 8 | 9 | 10 | 11 | 12 | 13 |
| 14 | 15 | 16 | 17 | 18 | 19 | 20 |
| 21 | 22 | 23 | 24 | 25 | 26 | 27 |
| 28 | 29 | 30 |   |   |   |   |

## Octubre

| M | T | W | T | F | S | S |
|---|---|---|---|---|---|---|
|   |   |   | 1 | 2 | 3 | 4 |
| 5 | 6 | 7 | 8 | 9 | 10 | 11 |
| 12 | 13 | 14 | 15 | 16 | 17 | 18 |
| 19 | 20 | 21 | 22 | 23 | 24 | 25 |
| 26 | 27 | 28 | 29 | 30 | 31 |   |

## Noviembre

| M | T | W | T | F | S | S |
|---|---|---|---|---|---|---|
|   |   |   |   |   |   | 1 |
| 2 | 3 | 4 | 5 | 6 | 7 | 8 |
| 9 | 10 | 11 | 12 | 13 | 14 | 15 |
| 16 | 17 | 18 | 19 | 20 | 21 | 22 |
| 23 | 24 | 25 | 26 | 27 | 28 | 29 |
| 30 |   |   |   |   |   |   |

## Diciembre

| M | T | W | T | F | S | S |
|---|---|---|---|---|---|---|
|   | 1 | 2 | 3 | 4 | 5 | 6 |
| 7 | 8 | 9 | 10 | 11 | 12 | 13 |
| 14 | 15 | 16 | 17 | 18 | 19 | 20 |
| 21 | 22 | 23 | 24 | 25 | 26 | 27 |
| 28 | 29 | 30 | 31 |   |   |   |

# AGOSTO

| DOMINGO | LUNES | MARTES | MIERCOLES |
|---------|-------|--------|-----------|
|  |  |  |  |
| 4 | 5 | 6 | 7 |
| 11 | 12 | 13 | 14 |
| 18 | 19 | 20 | 21 |
| 25 | 26 | 27 | 28 |

# 2019

| JUEVES | VIERNES | SABADO | NOTAS |
|---|---|---|---|
| 1 | 2 | 3 | |
| 8 | 9 | 10 | |
| 15 | 16 | 17 | |
| 22 | 23 | 24 | |
| 29 | 30 | 31 | |

# SEPTIEMBRE

| DOMINGO | LUNES | MARTES | MIERCOLES |
|---|---|---|---|
| 1 | 2 | 3 | 4 |
| 8 | 9 | 10 | 11 |
| 15 | 16 | 17 | 18 |
| 22 | 23 | 24 | 25 |
| 29 | 30 | | |

# 2019

| JUEVES | VIERNES | SABADO | NOTAS |
|---:|---:|---:|---|
| 5 | 6 | 7 | |
| 12 | 13 | 14 | |
| 19 | 20 | 21 | |
| 26 | 27 | 28 | |
| | | | |

# OCTUBRE

| DOMINGO | LUNES | MARTES | MIERCOLES |
|---------|-------|--------|-----------|
|  |  | 1 | 2 |
| 6 | 7 | 8 | 9 |
| 13 | 14 | 15 | 16 |
| 20 | 21 | 22 | 23 |
| 27 | 28 | 29 | 30 |

# 2019

| JUEVES | VIERNES | SABADO | NOTAS |
|---:|---:|---:|---|
| 3 | 4 | 5 | |
| 10 | 11 | 12 | |
| 17 | 18 | 19 | |
| 24 | 25 | 26 | |
| 31 | | | |

# NOVIEMBRE

| DOMINGO | LUNES | MARTES | MIERCOLES |
|---------|-------|--------|-----------|
|         |       |        |           |
| 3       | 4     | 5      | 6         |
| 10      | 11    | 12     | 13        |
| 17      | 18    | 19     | 20        |
| 24      | 25    | 26     | 27        |

# 2019

| JUEVES | VIERNES | SABADO | NOTAS |
|--------|---------|--------|-------|
|        | 1       | 2      |       |
| 7      | 8       | 9      |       |
| 14     | 15      | 16     |       |
| 21     | 22      | 23     |       |
| 28     | 29      | 30     |       |

# DICIEMBRE

| DOMINGO | LUNES | MARTES | MIERCOLES |
|---|---|---|---|
| 1 | 2 | 3 | 4 |
| 8 | 9 | 10 | 11 |
| 15 | 16 | 17 | 18 |
| 22 | 23 | 24 | 25 |
| 29 | 30 | 31 | |

# 2019

| JUEVES | VIERNES | SABADO | NOTAS |
|---:|---:|---:|---|
| 5 | 6 | 7 | |
| 12 | 13 | 14 | |
| 19 | 20 | 21 | |
| 26 | 27 | 28 | |
| | | | |

# ENERO

| DOMINGO | LUNES | MARTES | MIERCOLES |
|---------|-------|--------|-----------|
|         |       |        | 1         |
| 5       | 6     | 7      | 8         |
| 12      | 13    | 14     | 15        |
| 19      | 20    | 21     | 22        |
| 26      | 27    | 28     | 29        |

**2020**

| JUEVES | VIERNES | SABADO | NOTAS |
|---|---|---|---|
| 2 | 3 | 4 | |
| 9 | 10 | 11 | |
| 16 | 17 | 18 | |
| 23 | 24 | 25 | |
| 30 | 31 | | |

# FEBRERO

| DOMINGO | LUNES | MARTES | MIERCOLES |
|---------|-------|--------|-----------|
|         |       |        |           |
| 2       | 3     | 4      | 5         |
| 9       | 10    | 11     | 12        |
| 16      | 17    | 18     | 19        |
| 23      | 24    | 25     | 26        |

| JUEVES | VIERNES | SABADO | NOTAS |
|--------|---------|--------|-------|
|  |  | 1 |  |
| 6 | 7 | 8 |  |
| 13 | 14 | 15 |  |
| 20 | 21 | 22 |  |
| 27 | 28 | 29 |  |

# MARZO

| DOMINGO | LUNES | MARTES | MIERCOLES |
|---|---|---|---|
| 1 | 2 | 3 | 4 |
| 8 | 9 | 10 | 11 |
| 15 | 16 | 17 | 18 |
| 22 | 23 | 24 | 25 |
| 29 | 30 | 31 | |

# 2020

| JUEVES | VIERNES | SABADO | NOTAS |
|---|---|---|---|
| 5 | 6 | 7 | |
| 12 | 13 | 14 | |
| 19 | 20 | 21 | |
| 26 | 27 | 28 | |
| | | | |

# ABRIL

| DOMINGO | LUNES | MARTES | MIERCOLES |
|---------|-------|--------|-----------|
|         |       |        | 1         |
| 5       | 6     | 7      | 8         |
| 12      | 13    | 14     | 15        |
| 19      | 20    | 21     | 22        |
| 26      | 27    | 28     | 29        |

# 2 0 2 0

| JUEVES | VIERNES | SABADO | NOTAS |
|---|---|---|---|
| 2 | 3 | 4 | |
| 9 | 10 | 11 | |
| 16 | 17 | 18 | |
| 23 | 24 | 25 | |
| 30 | | | |

# MAYO

| DOMINGO | LUNES | MARTES | MIERCOLES |
|---------|-------|--------|-----------|
|         |       |        |           |
| 3       | 4     | 5      | 6         |
| 10      | 11    | 12     | 13        |
| 17      | 18    | 19     | 20        |
| 24/31   | 25    | 26     | 27        |

# 2020

| JUEVES | VIERNES | SABADO | NOTAS |
|---|---|---|---|
|  | 1 | 2 |  |
| 7 | 8 | 9 |  |
| 14 | 15 | 16 |  |
| 21 | 22 | 23 |  |
| 28 | 29 | 30 |  |

# JUNIO

| DOMINGO | LUNES | MARTES | MIERCOLES |
|---------|-------|--------|-----------|
|  | 1 | 2 | 3 |
| 7 | 8 | 9 | 10 |
| 14 | 15 | 16 | 17 |
| 21 | 22 | 23 | 24 |
| 28 | 29 | 30 |  |

# 2020

| JUEVES | VIERNES | SABADO | NOTAS |
|---|---|---|---|
| 4 | 5 | 6 | |
| 11 | 12 | 13 | |
| 18 | 19 | 20 | |
| 25 | 26 | 27 | |
| | | | |

# JULIO

| DOMINGO | LUNES | MARTES | MIERCOLES |
|---------|-------|--------|-----------|
|  |  |  | 1 |
| 5 | 6 | 7 | 8 |
| 12 | 13 | 14 | 15 |
| 19 | 20 | 21 | 22 |
| 26 | 27 | 28 | 29 |

# 2 0 1 9

| JUEVES | VIERNES | SABADO | NOTAS |
|--------|---------|--------|-------|
| 2 | 3 | 4 | |
| 9. | 10 | 11 | |
| 16 | 17 | 18 | |
| 23 | 24 | 25 | |
| 30 | 31 | | |

# Mi vision para el
## 2020

# Mis metas para el
# 2020

| | |
|---|---|
| 1 | |
| 2 | |
| 3 | |
| 4 | |
| 5 | |
| 6 | |
| 7 | |
| 8 | |
| 9 | |
| 10 | |

# CUMPLEAÑOS

| ENERO | FEBRERO | MARZO |
|---|---|---|
| | | |

| ABRIL | MAYO | JUNIO |
|---|---|---|
| | | |

| JULIO | AGOSTO | SEPTIEMBRE |
|---|---|---|
| | | |

| OCTUBRE | NOVIEMBRE | DICIEMBRE |
|---|---|---|
| | | |

# PASSWORDS

| WEB | USERNAME | PASSWORD |
|-----|----------|----------|
|     |          |          |
|     |          |          |
|     |          |          |
|     |          |          |
|     |          |          |
|     |          |          |
|     |          |          |
|     |          |          |

# PASSWORDS

| WEB | USERNAME | PASSWORD |
|-----|----------|----------|
|     |          |          |
|     |          |          |
|     |          |          |
|     |          |          |
|     |          |          |
|     |          |          |
|     |          |          |
|     |          |          |

# CONTACTOS

| NOMBRE | TELEFONO | EMAIL |
|--------|----------|-------|
|        |          |       |
|        |          |       |
|        |          |       |
|        |          |       |
|        |          |       |
|        |          |       |
|        |          |       |
|        |          |       |
|        |          |       |
|        |          |       |
|        |          |       |
|        |          |       |
|        |          |       |
|        |          |       |
|        |          |       |

# CONTACTOS

| NOMBRE | TELEFONO | EMAIL |
| --- | --- | --- |
| | | |
| | | |
| | | |
| | | |
| | | |
| | | |
| | | |
| | | |
| | | |
| | | |
| | | |
| | | |
| | | |
| | | |
| | | |

# Agosto

---

○ 29. LUNES

_____

_____

○ 30. MARTES

_____

_____

_____

_____

○ 31. MIERCOLES

COSAS QUE HACER:

_____

_____

○ 1. JUEVES

_____

_____

_____

_____

○ 2. VIERNES

_____

_____

_____

_____

○ 3. SABADO/ 4. DOMINGO

_____

_____

_____

# Agosto

○ 5. LUNES

○ 6. MARTES

○ 7. MIERCOLES

COSAS QUE HACER

○ 8. JUEVES

○ 9. VIERNES

○ 10. SABADO / 11.DOMINGO

# Agosto

○ 12. LUNES

**PRIORIDADES**

○ 13. MARTES

○ 14. MIERCOLES

**COSAS QUE HACER**

○ 15. JUEVES

○ 16. VIERNES

○ 17. SABADO / 18. DOMINGO

# Agosto

○ 19. LUNES

PRIORIDADES

○ 20. MARTES

○ 21. MIERCOLES

COSAS QUE HACER

○ 22. JUEVES

○ 23. VIERNES

○ 24. SABADO /25.DOMINGO

# Agosto Septiembre

---

○ 26. LUNES

**PRIORIDADES**

---
---
---

○ 27. MARTES

---
---
---
---

○ 28. MIERCOLES

**COSAS QUE HACER**

---
---

○ 29. JUEVES

---
---
---
---

○ 30. VIERNES

---
---
---
---

○ 31. SABADO / 1. DOMINGO

---
---
---

# Septiembre

○ 2. LUNES

**PRIORIDADES**

_____

_____

○ 3. MARTES

_____

_____

_____

_____

○ 4. MIERCOLES

**COSAS QUE HACER**

_____

_____

○ 5. JUEVES

_____

_____

_____

_____

○ 6. VIERNES

_____

_____

_____

_____

_____

○ 7. SABADO / 8.DOMINGO

_____

_____

_____

_____

# Septiembre

○ 9. LUNES

**PRIORIDADES**

○ 10. MARTES

○ 11. MIERCOLES

**COSAS QUE HACER**

○ 12. JUEVES

○ 13.VIERNES

○ 14. SABADO /15. DOMINGO

# Septiembre

○ 16. LUNES

PRIORIDADES

○ 17. MARTES

○ 18.MIERCOLES

COSAS QUE HACER

○ 19. JUEVES

○ 20. VIERNES

○ 21. SABADO /22. DOMINGO

# Septiembre

○ 23. LUNES

PRIORIDADES

○ 24. MARTES

○ 25. MIERCOLES

COSAS QUE HACER

○ 26. JUEVES

○ 27. VIERNES

○ 28. SABADO / 29. DOMINGO

# Octubre

○ 30. LUNES

**PRIORIDADES**

○ 1. MARTES

○ 2. MIERCOLES

**COSAS QUE HACER**

○ 3. JUEVES

○ 4. VIERNES

○ 5. SABADO / 6. DOMINGO

# Octubre

○ 7. LUNES

**PRIORIDADES**

○ 8. MARTES

○ 9. MIERCOLES

**COSAS QUE HACER**

○ 10. JUEVES

○ 11. VIERNES

○ 12. SABADO / 13. DOMINGO

# Octubre

○ 14. LUNES

**PRIORIDADES**

_____

○ 15. MARTES

_____

_____

_____

_____

○ 16. MIERCOLES

**COSAS QUE HACER**

_____

_____

○ 17. JUEVES

_____

_____

_____

○ 18. VIERNES

_____

_____

_____

_____

○ 19. SABADO / 20. DOMINGO

_____

_____

_____

_____

# Octubre

○ 21. LUNES

**PRIORIDADES**

○ 22. MARTES

○ 23. MIERCOLES

**COSAS QUE HACER**

○ 24. JUEVES

○ 25. VIERNES

○ 26. SABADO / 27. DOMINGO

# Noviembre

○ 28. LUNES

○ 29. MARTES

○ 30. MIERCOLES

COSAS QUE HACER

○ 31. JUEVES

○ 1. VIERNES

○ 2. SABADO / 3. DOMINGO

# Noviembre

○ 4. LUNES

○ 5. MARTES

○ 6. MIERCOLES

COSAS QUE HACER

○ 7. JUEVES

○ 8. VIERNES

○ 9. SABADO /10. DOMINGO

# Noviembre

○ 11. LUNES

**PRIORIDADES**

○ 12. MARTES

○ 13. MIERCOLES

**COSAS QUE HACER**

○ 14. JUEVES

○ 15. VIERNES

○ 16.SABADO /17. DOMINGO

# Noviembre

○ 18. LUNES

**PRIORIDADES**

○ 19. MARTES

○ 20. MIERCOLES

**COSAS QUE HACER**

○ 21. JUEVES

○ 22. VIERNES

○ 23. SABADO / 24. DOMINGO

# Noviembre Diciembre

○ 25. LUNES

**PRIORIDADES**

○ 26. MARTES

○ 27. MIERCOLES

**COSAS QUE HACER**

○ 28. JUEVES

○ 29. VIERNES

○ 30. SABADO / 1. DOMINGO

# Diciembre

---

○ 2. LUNES

PRIORIDADES

_____

_____

_____

○ 3. MARTES

_____

_____

_____

_____

○ 4. MIERCOLES

COSAS QUE HACER

_____

_____

_____

○ 5. JUEVES

_____

_____

_____

_____

○ 6. VIERNES

_____

_____

_____

_____

○ 7. SABADO /8. DOMINGO

_____

_____

_____

---

# Diciembre

○ 9. LUNES

**PRIORIDADES**

_____

_____

○ 10. MARTES

_____

_____

_____

_____

_____

○ 11. MIERCOLES

**COSAS QUE HACER**

_____

_____

○ 12. JUEVES

_____

_____

_____

_____

○ 13. VIERNES

_____

_____

_____

_____

○ 14. SABADO / 15. DOMINGO

_____

_____

_____

# Diciembre

○ 16. LUNES

○ 17. MARTES

○ 18. MIERCOLES

COSAS QUE HACER

○ 19. JUEVES

○ 20. VIERNES

○ 21. SABADO / 22. DOMINGO

# Diciembre

○ 23. LUNES

**PRIORIDADES**

_____

_____

○ 24. MARTES

_____

_____

_____

_____

○ 25. MIERCOLES

**COSAS QUE HACER**

_____

_____

○ 26. JUEVES

_____

_____

_____

_____

○ 27. VIERNES

_____

_____

_____

_____

○ 28. SABADO / 29. DOMINGO

_____

_____

_____

# Diciembre Enero

○ 30.  LUNES

○ 31. MARTES

○ 1. MIERCOLES

COSAS QUE HACER

○ 2. JUEVES

○ 3. VIERNES

○ 4. SABADO / 5. DOMINGO

# Enero

○ 6. LUNES

PRIORIDADES

○ 7. MARTES

○ 8. MIERCOLES

COSAS QUE HACER

○ 9. JUEVES

○ 10. VIERNES

○ 11. SABADO / 12. DOMINGO

# Enero

○ 13. LUNES

**PRIORIDADES**

○ 14. MARTES

○ 15. MIERCOLES

**COSAS QUE HACER**

○ 16. JUEVES

○ 17. VIERNES

○ 18. SABADO / 19. DOMINGO

# Enero

---

○ 20. LUNES

PRIORIDADES

_____

_____

_____

○ 21. MARTES

_____

_____

_____

_____

○ 22. MIERCOLES

COSAS QUE HACER

_____

_____

_____

○ 23. JUEVES

_____

_____

_____

_____

○ 24. VIERNES

_____

_____

_____

_____

○ 25. SABADO / 26. DOMINGO

_____

_____

_____

# Enero Febrero

○ 27. LUNES

**PRIORIDADES**

○ 28. MARTES

○ 29. MIERCOLES

**COSAS QUE HACER**

○ 30. JUEVES

○ 31. VIERNES

○ 1.SABADO / 2. DOMINGO

# Febrero

○ 3. LUNES

PRIORIDADES

○ 4. MARTES

○ 5. MIERCOLES

COSAS QUE HACER

○ 6. JUEVES

○ 7. VIERNES

○ 8. SABADO /9. DOMINGO

# Febrero

○ 10. LUNES

PRIORIDADES

○ 11. MARTES

○ 12. MIERCOLES

COSAS QUE HACER

○ 13. JUEVES

○ 14. VIERNES

○ 15. SABADO /16. DOMINGO

# Febrero

○ 17. LUNES

○ 18. MARTES

○ 19. MIERCOLES

COSAS QUE HACER

○ 20. JUEVES

○ 21. VIERNES

○ 22. SABADO / 23. DOMINGO

# Febrero Marzo

○ 24. LUNES

**PRIORIDADES**

○ 25. MARTES

○ 26. MIERCOLES

**COSAS QUE HACER**

○ 27. JUEVES

○ 28. VIERNES

○ 29. SABADO / 1. DOMINGO

# Marzo

○ 2. LUNES

PRIORIDADES

○ 3. MARTES

○ 4. MIERCOLES

COSAS QUE HACER

○ 5. JUEVES

○ 6. VIERNES

○ 7.SABADO / 8. DOMINGO

# Marzo

○ 9. LUNES

**PRIORIDADES**

○ 10. MARTES

○ 11. MIERCOLES

**COSAS QUE HACER**

○ 12. JUEVES

○ 13. VIERNES

○ 14. SABADO / 15. DOMINGO

# Marzo

---

○ 16. LUNES

PRIORIDADES

_____
_____
_____

○ 17. MARTES

_____
_____
_____

○ 18. MIERCOLES

COSAS QUE HACER

_____
_____

○ 19. JUEVES

_____
_____
_____
_____

○ 20. VIERNES

_____
_____
_____

○ 21.SABADO / 22. DOMINGO

_____
_____
_____

# Marzo

○ 23. LUNES

PRIORIDADES

_____

_____

_____

○ 24. MARTES

_____

_____

_____

○ 25. MIERCOLES

COSAS QUE HACER

_____

_____

○ 26. JUEVES

_____

_____

_____

_____

○ 27. VIERNES

_____

_____

_____

_____

○ 28.SABADO / 29. DOMINGO

_____

_____

_____

# Marzo Abril

○ 30. LUNES

PRIORIDADES

○ 31. MARTES

○ 1. MIERCOLES

COSAS QUE HACER

○ 2. JUEVES

○ 3. VIERNES

○ 4.SABADO / 5. DOMINGO

# Abril

○ 6. LUNES

**PRIORIDADES**

○ 7. MARTES

○ 8. MIERCOLES

**COSAS QUE HACER**

○ 9. JUEVES

○ 10. VIERNES

○ 11. SABADO / 12. DOMINGO

# Abril

○ 13. LUNES

○ 14. MARTES

○ 15. MIERCOLES

COSAS QUE HACER

○ 16. JUEVES

○ 17. VIERNES

○ 18. SABADO / 19. DOMINGO

# Abril

○ 20. LUNES

**PRIORIDADES**

_____

_____

○ 21. MARTES

_____

_____

_____

_____

○ 22. MIERCOLES

**COSAS QUE HACER**

_____

_____

○ 23. JUEVES

_____

_____

_____

_____

○ 24. VIERNES

_____

_____

_____

_____

○ 25. SABADO / 26. DOMINGO

_____

_____

_____

# Abril Mayo

○ 27. LUNES

PRIORIDADES

○ 28. MARTES

○ 29. MIERCOLES

COSAS QUE HACER

○ 30. JUEVES

○ 1. VIERNES

○ 2. SABADO / 3. DOMINGO

# Mayo

○ 4. LUNES

**PRIORIDADES**

○ 5. MARTES

○ 6. MIERCOLES

**COSAS QUE HACER**

○ 7. JUEVES

○ 8. VIERNES

○ 9.SABADO / 10. DOMINGO

# Mayo

○ 11. LUNES

**PRIORIDADES**

○ 12. MARTES

○ 13. MIERCOLES

**COSAS QUE HACER**

○ 14. JUEVES

○ 15. VIERNES

○ 16. SABADO / 17. DOMINGO

# Mayo

○ 18. LUNES

PRIORIDADES

○ 19. MARTES

○ 20. MIERCOLES

COSAS QUE HACER

○ 21. JUEVES

○ 22. VIERNES

○ 23. SABADO /24. DOMINGO

# Mayo

○ 25. LUNES

**PRIORIDADES**

○ 26. MARTES

○ 27. MIERCOLES

**COSAS QUE HACER**

○ 28. JUEVES

○ 29. VIERNES

○ 30. SABADO / 31. DOMINGO

# Junio

○ 1. LUNES

**PRIORIDADES**

○ 2. MARTES

○ 3. MIERCOLES

**COSAS QUE HACER**

○ 4. JUEVES

○ 5. VIERNES

○ 6. SABADO / 7. DOMINGO

# Junio

○ 8. LUNES

PRIORIDADES

○ 9. MARTES

○ 10. MIERCOLES

COSAS QUE HACER

○ 11. JUEVES

○ 12. VIERNES

○ 13. SABADO / 14. DOMINGO

# Junio

○ 15. LUNES

**PRIORIDADES**

○ 16. MARTES

○ 17. MIERCOLES

**COSAS QUE HACER**

○ 18. JUEVES

○ 19. VIERNES

○ 20. SABADO / 21. DOMINGO

# Junio

○ 22. LUNES

○ 23. MARTES

○ 24. MIERCOLES

COSAS QUE HACER

○ 25. JUEVES

○ 26. VIERNES

○ 27. SABADO / 28. DOMINGO

# Junio Julio

○ 29. LUNES

○ 30. MARTES

○ 1. MIERCOLES

COSAS QUE HACER

○ 2. JUEVES

○ 3. VIERNES

○ 4. SABADO / 5. DOMINGO

# Julio

○ 6. LUNES

**PRIORIDADES**

_____
_____
_____
_____
_____

○ 7. MARTES

_____
_____

○ 8. MIERCOLES

**COSAS QUE HACER**

_____
_____

○ 9. JUEVES

_____
_____
_____

○ 10. VIERNES

_____
_____
_____
_____
_____

○ 11. SABADO / 12. DOMINGO

_____
_____
_____
_____

# Julio

○ 13. LUNES

**PRIORIDADES**

○ 14. MARTES

○ 15. MIERCOLES

**COSAS QUE HACER**

○ 16. JUEVES

○ 17. VIERNES

○ 18. SABADO / 19 . DOMINGO

# Julio

○ 20. LUNES

○ 21. MARTES

○ 22. MIERCOLES

COSAS QUE HACER

○ 23. JUEVES

○ 24. VIERNES

○ 25. SABADO / 26. DOMINGO

# Julio

○ 27. LUNES

○ 28. MARTES

○ 29. MIERCOLES

COSAS QUE HACER

○ 30. JUEVES

○ 31. VIERNES

○ 1.SABADO / 2. DOMINGO

# NOTAS

www.ingramcontent.com/pod-product-compliance
Lightning Source LLC
Chambersburg PA
CBHW070431290526
45791CB00005B/1921